SECRETS
OF AMERICAN
WORLD

Secret Agents! Sharks! Ghost Armies!

by Laurie Calkhoven

illustrated by Valerio Fabbretti

Ready-to-Read

Simon Spotlight
New York London Toronto Sydney New Delhi

Note to Parents: While we strive to provide age-appropriate content, we felt that it would be unjust to discuss any aspect of World War II without referencing some of the atrocities committed during that time period. This book offers an entry point for these discussions but is not intended to be a detailed recounting of those horrific events.

SIMON SPOTLIGHT
An imprint of Simon & Schuster Children's Publishing Division
1230 Avenue of the Americas, New York, New York 10020
This Simon Spotlight edition July 2017
Text copyright © 2017 by Simon & Schuster, Inc.
Illustrations copyright © 2017 by Valerio Fabbretti
All rights reserved, including the right of reproduction in whole or in part in any form.
SIMON SPOTLIGHT, READY-TO-READ, and colophon are registered trademarks of Simon & Schuster, Inc.
For information about special discounts for bulk purchases, please contact Simon & Schuster Special Sales at
1-866-506-1949 or business@simonandschuster.com.
Manufactured in the United States of America 0517 LAK
2 4 6 8 10 9 7 5 3 1
This book has been cataloged with the Library of Congress.
ISBN 978-1-4814-9949-1 (hc)
ISBN 978-1-4814-9948-4 (pbk)
ISBN 978-1-4814-9950-7 (eBook)

Contents

Chapter 1
World War II Begins

What comes to mind when you think about World War II? Maybe you think about tanks and soldiers, fighter planes and big battles. But what if we told you that World War II was also about shark repellent and secret laboratories, cunning disguises and thrilling adventures?

Sometimes winning a war is about more than the size of a country's army or how well equipped its soldiers are. Sometimes winning a war is about creativity—coming up with clever ways to stay one step ahead of the enemy.

The people in this book did all that and more, and some of them had to keep their part in the war secret for many, many years. Are you ready to hear their stories? If so, read on to unlock the secrets of American history!

World War II lasted from 1939 to 1945 and was fought in nearly every part of the world.

The war began on September 1, 1939, when Germany invaded Poland. But to find out why Germany invaded, we have to look back even farther. When Germany lost World War I in 1918, the country had to give up land and power. It also had to pay back other countries for the costs of the war.

Many German people thought that was unfair, and blamed their problems on the Jewish people. One such person was Adolf Hitler, the head of the Nazi political party who later became the leader of Germany.

He promised he would make Germany the most powerful country in Europe.

Led by Hitler, the Nazis did terrible things. They persecuted—or even killed—anyone they considered different. In Germany and elsewhere they stole land and valuables from citizens, forced them to work for free, and put them in concentration camps against their will. Twelve million or more people were killed as a result of these actions, called the Holocaust, including six million Jewish people. It was all part of Hitler's horrible plan.

At the same time that Hitler wanted to control Europe, Japan wanted to take over Asia. The two countries agreed to help each other. Italy also joined them. They were known as the Axis powers. With Italy's help, Germany took over many countries in Europe, and Japan took over some countries in Asia and the Pacific Ocean.

Great Britain, France, and the Soviet Union fought against the Axis powers. They were known as the Allied powers or the Allies.

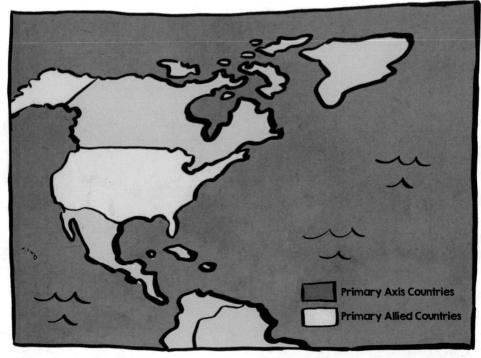

Primary Axis Countries

Primary Allied Countries

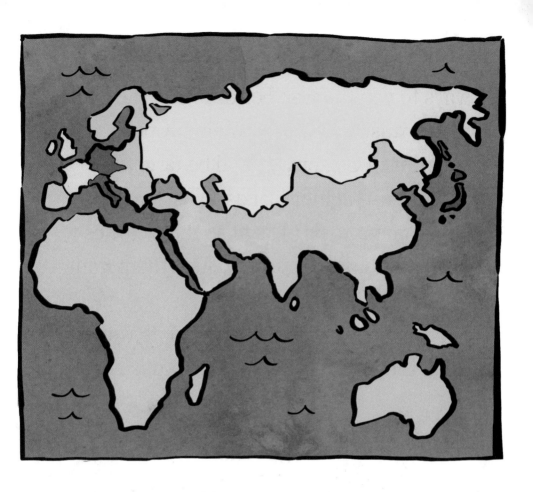

The United States tried to help by sending weapons and food to Great Britain. But many Americans wanted to stay out of the fight at first.

Then, on December 7, 1941, Japan attacked the US Naval Base at Pearl Harbor in Hawaii. Suddenly America was at war. The United States became one of the Allies.

The Allies had to come up with creative ways to win the war. For example, the United States was worried that their weapons factories in California could be targeted by Japanese fighter planes. What was the government to do? Disguise the factories to look like something else to hide them from the enemy!

From up in the sky, enemy pilots would think they were flying over an ordinary town.

It was actually tarps painted to look like a town! Those tarps hid a factory so it could keep making fighter jets.

That's just one of the many clever, courageous, and daring ways Americans fought the Axis powers!

Chapter 2
Cooking Up Shark Repellent

Imagine that you're a fighter pilot or a navy sailor and your plane or ship has broken down or been damaged in battle. If you were stranded in the middle of the ocean with nothing but your life vest, waiting for a rescue ship to arrive, what might scare you?

Many sailors and pilots were scared of sharks!

It wasn't just sailors and pilots who had to worry about sharks. The United States planted mines underwater to keep German and Italian submarines away from our ships. But curious sharks bumped up against the mines, and—*KABOOM!* The mines exploded.

The United States had to do something about the shark problem. That's where the Office of Strategic Services (OSS) came in. The OSS later became the Central Intelligence Agency, or CIA, which is a spy agency.

During the war, the OSS sent spies into enemy countries and cracked enemy codes. They also worked to come up with creative solutions to big problems.

One of the people working on a solution to the shark problem was Julia Child. Many years after the war, Julia became a world-famous chef. She taught Americans how to cook French food through cookbooks and TV shows. But at that time in the 1940s, Julia just wanted to help the United States win the war.

She tried to join the military, but back then women had to be between five and six feet tall to enlist. Julia was six feet two inches tall. So she moved to

Washington, DC, and got a job with the OSS. Her assignment was to create a recipe for something that even sharks wouldn't eat.

"My first big recipe was shark repellent that I mixed in a bathtub for the navy, for the men who might get caught in the water," Julia later said.

Julia and a team at the OSS tested more than a hundred different recipes to keep sharks away. Finally they hit on something that seemed to work—a chemical called copper acetate. To sharks, it smelled like a dead shark.

The OSS spent many months testing what they called Shark Chaser. Then the navy started smearing it on their underwater mines. Sailors and pilots wore little cakes of it on their belts or strapped to their arms. When the cakes hit the water, they started to dissolve. The hope was that the Shark Chaser would keep sharks away for six to seven hours.

Did Shark Chaser really work? Probably not as well as the OSS hoped. Even so, the military used the recipe for more than thirty years. There was just one more problem: it didn't keep away other deadly fish, like barracuda and piranhas. Yikes!

Chapter 3
The Ghost Army with the Inflatable Tanks

Okay, so the Ghost Army wasn't really made up of ghosts. The Ghost Army was called that because it was a small unit that seemed to have many more soldiers than it actually did. The soldiers were also able to appear and disappear quickly. How did they do that? We're glad you asked!

The 23rd Headquarters Special Troops was a top secret unit of the US army made up of 1,100 artists, architects, and engineers. This Ghost Army fooled Hitler and the German army in more than twenty missions. One way they did this was by making it appear as though the Ghost Army was a much larger unit, with tens of thousands of soldiers.

The Ghost Army placed fake inflatable tanks and airplanes near real ones in camps they knew the Germans would see. The Germans thought the United States was getting ready for a huge attack, but the real attack would take place miles away.

The Ghost Army also drove trucks with huge speakers into French forests and used them to blast sound recordings made back home in Fort Knox, Kentucky, of US soldiers and tanks on the move. The recordings could be heard from fifteen miles away. They fooled the enemy into thinking that the woods were patrolled by thousands of soldiers and tanks. It was really just a few men and speakers on the back of a few trucks.

But that's not all. Soldiers in the Ghost Army would stroll into cafés and talk about fake battle plans. They did that in places where German spies would be listening. They also created fake radio broadcasts for the Germans to listen in on.

Why were all these tricks important?
If the Germans overheard a conversation
or radio broadcast that made them think
Americans were preparing an attack in
the north, the Germans would move their
troops there to defend the area. But that
left other areas undefended. The Allies
would send troops to *those* areas to take
control of the region quickly.

The Ghost Army also helped hide the movements of other army units. While another unit would move on to a different location, the Ghost Army would stay behind in plain sight of the Germans. This made it look like the area was still heavily defended.

But the Ghost Army's biggest trick took place in 1945, near the end of the war. The US army was ready to cross the Rhine River into Germany. The Ghost Army's job was to make the German army believe that US troops would cross the river miles away from where they would actually cross.

The Ghost Army placed fake tanks beside real ones. They played sound recordings of soldiers building bridges. They made it look like there were 20,000 soldiers there instead of 1,100.

The tactics worked! The German army moved in to fight the Ghost Army. That gave the much larger unit of US troops the chance to cross the river far away, where they only had to battle a few German soldiers!

The Ghost Army's work saved thousands and thousands of lives, but it was also top secret. It wasn't until 1996 that the United States told the world about the Ghost Army.

What other World War II secrets might still be hidden away?

Chapter 4
The Allies' Most Dangerous Spy

When you think about spies, what comes to mind? Disguises, secret messages, or maybe an exciting chase? The story of the Allies' most dangerous spy has all that and more!

Her name was Virginia Hall, and she became a hero in World War II. Born in Maryland in 1906, she grew to love languages and adventure. After college, Virginia got jobs at different US embassies in Europe. She wanted to join the foreign service, a branch of the government that represents the United States in countries around the world.

In 1933, Virginia lost her lower left leg in a hunting accident. A doctor gave her a wooden leg to help her walk. She named her leg Cuthbert.

At the time, the US government had strict laws that prevented people with disabilities from working in the foreign service. Unfortunately, Virginia had to find a new career.

When the war broke out in Europe, Virginia was in France. She volunteered to drive an ambulance. It was a hard and dangerous job.

When France was taken over by Germany, Virginia went to England. She volunteered to be a spy for Great Britain.

The British spy agency sent Virginia back to France. She pretended to be a newspaper reporter, but her real mission was to set up a spy network. The network would collect valuable information, help Allied prisoners of war escape the Nazis, and get supplies to people who needed them.

Before long, the Germans started to catch on to Virginia. They called her the "Lady with a Limp" and put up wanted posters all over France. They offered a reward for her capture. Virginia had to escape!

She hiked over the steep mountains between France and Spain to get away. Spain was not under Axis control.

It was a long trip, and the Germans were right behind her! Virginia's wooden leg slowed her down, but she made it to Spain. Soon after, she returned to England.

The British spy agency wouldn't send Virginia into France again because the Germans were still looking for her. Remember the OSS, the American spy agency? By this time the United States had joined the war, so Virginia was able to sign up as a spy for the OSS. She dyed her hair gray and dressed like an old woman so that the Germans wouldn't recognize her, and she snuck back into France.

By day, Virginia worked on French farms as a milkmaid.

By night, she taught the French how to sabotage, or destroy, the German soldiers' plans. Her team blew up four bridges and stopped freight trains to keep the Germans from transporting supplies, ammunition, and troops! Virginia also sent coded radio messages to let the

Americans know what the German troops were doing.

Virginia's missions took her all over France. She stayed on the move, camping out in barns and attics. Even by the end of the war, the Germans never caught the woman they considered to be the Allies' most dangerous spy.

After the war, Virginia Hall was given the Distinguished Service Cross by the head of the OSS. She was the only American civilian woman to receive this important honor during World War II.

World War II was one of the largest wars ever fought. Germany, Italy, and Japan wanted to take over the world. For the US and the Allies, the war was a fight for freedom.

Many Americans got involved and did their best to help. Some of them grew their own vegetables in "victory gardens" so that farm goods could be shipped to the troops, or they recycled rubber and tin to help the military build tanks and airplanes.

Still more came up with creative ideas to fool the enemy, while others volunteered to fight on the front lines.

Without the bravery and creativity of everyday Americans, the world would look very different today.

Read on to learn more about the secrets of American history, and some science, math, and social studies along the way!

Sharks: At the Top of the Food Chain

When you think about sharks, you might say that they're cool or scary or powerful, but sharks are more than just that: they're important. Sharks are a vital part of the ocean's food chain.

A **food chain** is a way of grouping together animals and plants by what they eat and what they are eaten by.

In the ocean's food chain, the first, or bottom, level is phytoplankton. Phytoplankton (FIGHT-oh-plank-ton) are tiny plants that float near the surface of the ocean. They use sunlight, water, and carbon dioxide to make their own food through a process known as photosynthesis (foh-toh-SIN-theh-sis), just like land-based plants. Because they make, or produce, their own food, phytoplankton are known as **producers.**

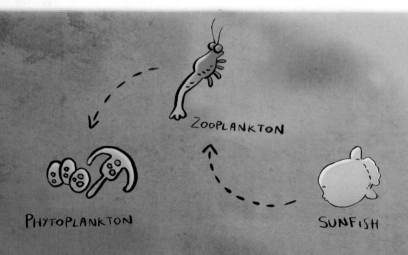

ZOOPLANKTON

PHYTOPLANKTON

SUNFISH

On the next level of the food chain are tiny animals called zooplankton (ZOH-oh-plank-ton). Zooplankton are called **consumers** because they eat phytoplankton. Zooplankton are then eaten by bigger consumers, such as sunfish. Sunfish are eaten by larger fish, such as mackerel, which are eaten by even larger fish, like tuna.

At the top of the food chain are large animals like sharks. Sharks are called **apex predators** because no animals in their environment usually eat them. What makes sharks so important? Without them, the food chain would become unbalanced. In other words, if there were no sharks around to eat the tuna, then there would be too many tuna in the ocean, which would then affect smaller fish like mackerel, and so on down.

So give sharks some fin—they're an important part of the food chain!

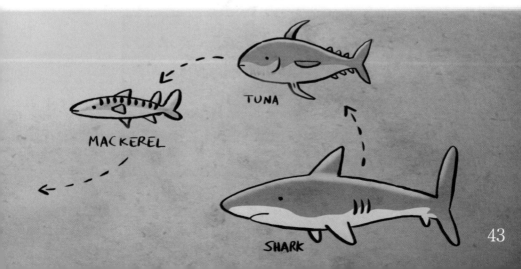

MACKEREL

TUNA

SHARK

Measuring Area

Area is the size of a surface. You can use it to measure the land needed to build a house, to find the right size pool for your backyard, or even to figure out the size of an entire country. Area is important for builders and engineers, but it's also important for the military when they're getting ready for a mission.

Area is calculated differently depending on the shape that is being measured. When you're measuring the area of a rectangle, you multiply **length** (how long the rectangle is) by **width** (how wide the rectangle is). If you measure that rectangle in feet, the resulting area is called **square feet**. See if you can use area to solve the following math problem!

To throw off the Germans, the Ghost Army is setting up inflatable tanks in a field. The field is 90 feet long and 80 feet wide. The inflatable tanks are each 20 feet long and 9 feet wide. How many inflatable tanks can the Ghost Army put in the field?

LENGTH

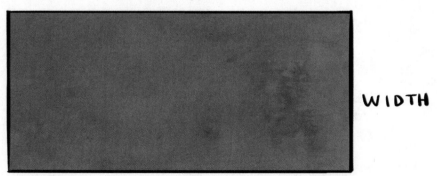

WIDTH

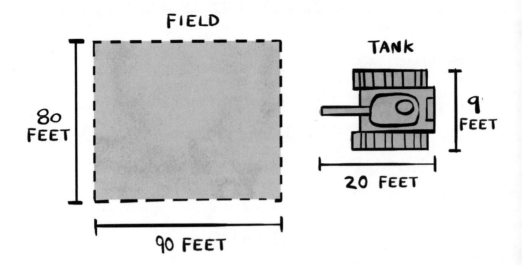

FIELD

80 FEET

90 FEET

TANK

9 FEET

20 FEET

To solve this problem, we have to find the area of the field:

length x width = area
90 feet long x 80 feet wide = 7,200 square feet

Next, we have to find the area of one tank:

length x width = area
20 feet long x 9 feet wide = 180 square feet

Now that we know the area of the field (7,200 square feet) and the area of one tank (180 square feet), all we have to do is find out how many times 180 (each tank) can go into 7,200 (area of field). Another way to say that is, what is 7,200 divided by 180?

7,200 square feet ÷ 180 square feet = 40

This means that the Ghost Army can set up 40 tanks in the field! Isn't area great?

Famous People Were Also Spies!

If you thought Virginia Hall was amazing, there are even more incredible spies from World War II for you to meet. Here are two of them you might recognize! Did you know that even children's book authors and performers helped with the war effort?

Roald Dahl

Roald Dahl, author of *Matilda*, *Charlie and the Chocolate Factory*, and many other books, was a fighter pilot for the British. After he was injured, he became a spy. Surprisingly, Roald wasn't sent to spy on the enemy—he came to the United States to spy for Great Britain! Before the attack on Pearl Harbor, when many American people were against getting involved in the war, Britain ran a secret spy ring whose goal was to convince the United States to fight on their side during World War II. Roald's mission was to convince wealthy and powerful Americans to support the war effort.

Josephine Baker

Josephine Baker was a famous African American jazz singer and dancer . . . but she was also a spy! In America, Josephine faced a lot of discrimination because of her race. But in the early 1920s, after performing in dancing troupes and Broadway musicals, Josephine traveled to Paris, France. Her incredible dancing, stunning beauty, and outspoken personality made her one of the most popular performers in Europe!

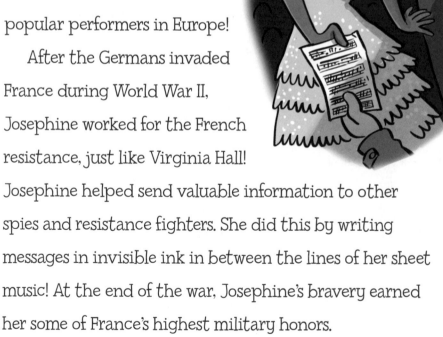

After the Germans invaded France during World War II, Josephine worked for the French resistance, just like Virginia Hall! Josephine helped send valuable information to other spies and resistance fighters. She did this by writing messages in invisible ink in between the lines of her sheet music! At the end of the war, Josephine's bravery earned her some of France's highest military honors.

ARE YOU FEELING BRAVE?

TAKE THE SECRET AGENTS! SHARKS! GHOST ARMIES! QUIZ!

1. What year did World War II officially begin?

a. 2001   b. 1939   c. 1219

2. What did Germany, Japan, and Italy call themselves?

a. Axis powers   b. Allied powers   c. Super powers

3. What was one reason the OSS wanted to make shark repellent?

a. Sharks smell bad.   b. Sharks were   c. Sharks were
                          destroying submarines.   causing underwater
                                                   mines to explode.

4. What was the chemical Julia Child and her team used in their shark repellent?

a. copper acetate   b. hydrogen dioxide   c. orange juice

5. During the end of the war, the Ghost Army helped another army unit cross which river into Germany?

a. Nile River   b. Amazon River   c. Rhine River

6. Both Virginia Hall and Julia Child were members of the OSS, which later became . . .

a. the army   b. the CIA   c. the Secret Service

7. What was Virginia Hall awarded at the end of World War II?

a. Purple Heart   b. Medal of Honor   c. Distinguished Service Cross

8. What is a big animal like a shark known as in a food chain?

a. producer   b. apex predator   c. baloney

Answers: 1.b 2.a 3.c 4.a 5.c 6.b 7.c 8.b